A
ROMAN
FORT

Series Editor	David Salariya
Book Editor	Jenny Millington
Consultant	Stephen Johnson

Author:
Fiona Macdonald studied history at Cambridge University and at the University of East Anglia, where she is now a part-time tutor in Medieval History. She has written many books on historical topics, mainly for children.

Illustrator:
Gerald Wood was born in London and began his career in film advertising. He then illustrated magazines for many years before becoming a book illustrator specialising in historical reconstruction.

Consultant:
Stephen Johnson studied Classics and Archaeology at Oxford University, concentrating on Roman fortifications. He has written several books on Roman forts, and on Roman Britain, including one on Hadrian's Wall. Since 1984 he has worked for English Heritage as an Archaeologist, Publisher, and most recently as a Regional Director.

Created, designed and produced by
The Salariya Book Co Ltd, Brighton, UK.

First published in 1993
by Simon & Schuster Young Books
Campus 400
Maylands Avenue
Hemel Hempstead
Herts
HP2 7EZ

ISBN 0-7500-1338-9

A catalogue record for this book is available from the British Library.

Printed and bound in Hong Kong by Wing King Tong Ltd.

INSIDE STORY

A ROMAN FORT

FIONA MACDONALD   GERALD WOOD

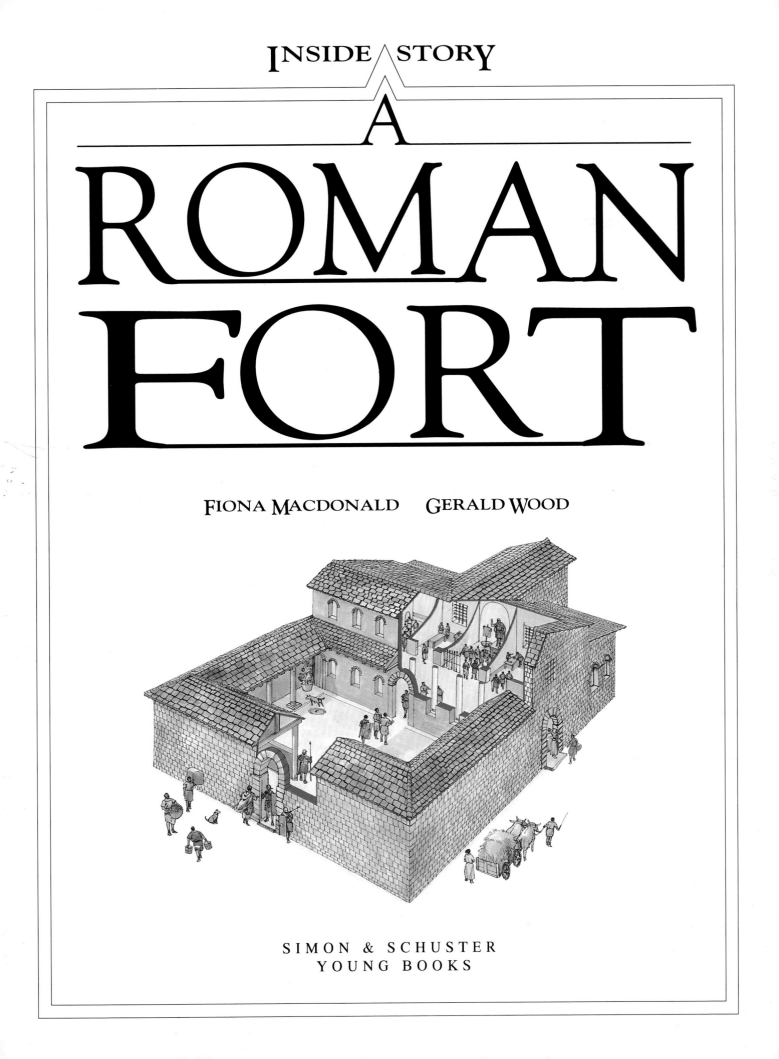

SIMON & SCHUSTER
YOUNG BOOKS

CONTENTS

INTRODUCTION

'Let it be your task, Roman, to control the nations with your power.' That is what one Roman poet wrote, around 19 BC. During the years covered by this book (from about 50 BC to AD 200), Rome ruled over the largest empire in the world, with borders stretching for thousands of miles. The empire's frontiers were guarded by a magnificent army. While on duty, Roman soldiers lived in tents in camps, or set up permanent bases in strongly-built forts.

We can still see and admire the remains of many of these forts today. Some of the best preserved examples can be found close to Hadrian's Wall in northern England, although forts were also built in Germany, North Africa, Transylvania (modern-day Romania), the Middle East, Scotland and Wales. Why were forts necessary? Who designed and built them? What was it like to live inside one? And how were forts defended when Rome's enemies attacked?

Fortunately, we have plenty of surviving evidence to help us answer these questions. Archaeologists have excavated the sites of many Roman forts, and have discovered not only traces of long-lost buildings, but also thousands of objects made or used by the people who lived there. Roman writers have left descriptions of how forts were built, as well as histories of military campaigns. And in Rome, a marvellous series of pictures carved on a tall monument, known as Trajan's Column, provides us with a very detailed picture of Roman army life.

THE ROMAN EMPIRE

In AD 117, the Roman empire was at its height. It extended across an enormous territory, from southern Scotland to the Caspian Sea. All conquered lands sent goods and money to Rome, as tribute and taxes. In return, Roman government officials and Roman soldiers stationed all around the empire claimed to bring peace, good laws and profitable trade. Conquered peoples did not always take this view of what was going on. As one British chieftain was reported to have said: 'What they call empire-building is just plundering, butchering and theft; they make a desert, and call it "peace".'

Rome had not always been powerful. But around 510 BC, it began to develop from a small town into a busy city. Roman citizens fought – successfully – to control vital trade routes throughout southern Italy, and for space to build new temples, houses and farms.

After about 270 BC, Roman troops began to conquer neighbouring lands. By 30 BC, they controlled most of the countries bordering the Mediterranean Sea. Roman generals also looked further afield for conquests and marched northwards into Switzerland, Germany and France. They arrived in Britain in AD 43, and overran most of the Middle East between AD 106-116. Roman imperial power lasted for almost five centuries, finally collapsing in about AD 476.

The earliest Roman money (1) showed pictures of valuable goods. Coins made before c.100 BC (2-3) showed figures from myths. After that, Roman rulers issued coins (4-9) advertising themselves and their achievements.

GERMANY

BRITAIN

FRANCE

Atlantic Ocean

SPAIN

In Roman times, the countries of Europe we know today did not exist. Instead, Europe was divided into many smaller states. Each was the homeland of a different tribe. On this map (left), you can see the names of states in Roman Europe.

The Roman empire (below) grew rich through taxes, but also through trade. Roman merchants made business deals with local suppliers throughout the empire, and so a great many rare and valuable goods came to Rome from distant lands, and were sold to wealthy customers in the markets there.

Germania
Britannia
Dacia
Italia
Judea
Cyrenaica
Aegyptus
Africa

Caspian Sea
ROMANIA
Black Sea
TURKEY
GREECE
ITALY
EGYPT
Mediterranean Sea
AFRICA

N
E
W
S

KEY

pottery		copper	
wool		lead	
cloth		tin	
wine		papyrus	
olive oil		honey	
fruit		glass	
wheat		leather or pelts	
gold		marble	
silver		iron	

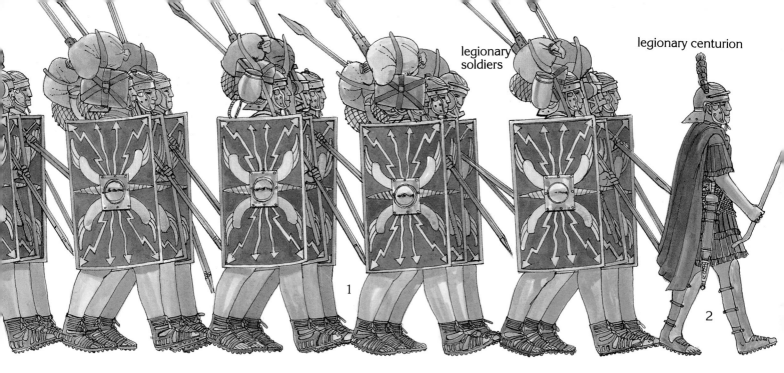

legionary soldiers

legionary centurion

1

2

THE ROMAN ARMY

Rome's astonishing conquests would have been impossible without an efficient, loyal army. Under the empire, the Roman army became the first full-time, professional fighting force in the world. (Before then, it consisted of ordinary Roman citizens, who served part-time.) These professionals were always ready for war. The historian Josephus wrote in AD 64, 'They do not wait for war to begin before getting to grips with their weapons, nor are they idle in peacetime... but, as if born with weapons in their hands, they never stop training...'.

Each group of 80 foot-soldiers (1) was led by a centurion (2). Other officers included standard-bearers (3) who also acted as treasurers and pay-masters. They were accompanied into battle by specially-

It was the army's task to guard the frontiers of Rome's mighty empire. In some cases, this did not involve much fighting. Where the local leaders accepted Roman government, as they did in parts of Africa, only a token 'police force' of Roman troops was needed. In other regions of the empire, such as Britain, France and Germany, Roman rule was bitterly opposed. As a result, Roman soldiers stationed there often had to fight for their lives.

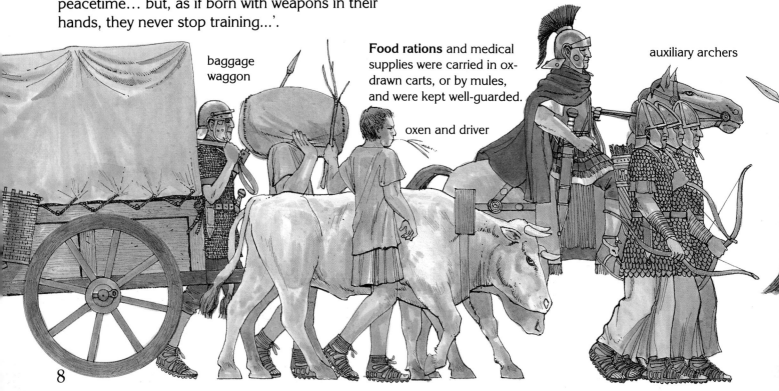

baggage waggon

Food rations and medical supplies were carried in ox-drawn carts, or by mules, and were kept well-guarded.

oxen and driver

auxiliary archers

standards

legionary bodyguards

6

commander
of the legion

3　　4　　5

trained musicians (4), who
sounded orders on loud
brass trumpets. The senior
standard-bearer (5) wore

the skin of his legion's
totem animal, such as a
wolf or boar. He kept close
to the commander (6).

A **Roman legion** (below) was divided into a number of
smaller units. This made it easier to organise and control,
and also helped officers to arrange their men most
effectively on the battlefield.

The Roman imperial army contained about
150,000 regular soldiers, called legionaries, plus
their officers and commanders. For the
legionaries, the army was a life-long career. They
signed on for 25 years' service, and, inevitably,
many died before it was time to retire. At first,
legionaries were recruited only from the citizens
of Rome, but after c.100 BC, men from all
Roman lands were encouraged to enlist. As well
as legionary troops, the Roman army included
auxiliary soldiers (see page 10), who provided
specialists like archers and riders.

How a legion was divided:

8 men = 1 contubernium (tent-group)	2 centuries	= 1 maniple
	6 centuries	= 1 cohort
10 contubernia = 1 century	10 cohorts	= 1 legion

auxiliary
foot-soldiers

auxiliary
cavalry
officer

standard

auxiliary
standard
bearer

auxiliary
centurion

OTHER FORCES

Auxiliary soldiers were originally recruited from non-Roman nations. Their name means 'helpers', and they were meant to assist Roman legionary troops by providing either extra manpower or specialised fighting techniques. Auxiliaries fought using the weapons and armour of their native lands: archers with bows and arrows came from the Middle East; men used to fighting on horseback came from conquered tribes in France; and sling-shot throwers, armed with lethal stone 'bullets', came from the southern Mediterranean. But before long there was little practical difference, apart from their weapons, between legionary and auxiliary troops. The government in Rome relied on both groups of soldiers to defend its vast empire.

A Roman soldier, on horseback and armed with a spear, fighting against Celtic enemies in Gaul (present-day France). This carving comes from a Roman stone sarcophagus (coffin) found in Italy.

When soldiers or sailors retired from active service, they were given certificates to record the rewards they had earned. So that they would last, these certificates were often cast in bronze.

Roman warships were powered by men rowing. They were steered using two enormous paddles.

drummer sounding orders

A typical warship was about 45 metres long and 9 metres wide. It carried about 600 fighting troops, and was crewed by 250 extra sailors or slaves.

army officers

steering paddle

Army commanders were chosen from young men born to noble families. After

good schooling, they made a career in public service, first serving as senators and

then as magistrates in one of the empire's provinces. If they worked wisely, they

were chosen by the emperor to serve as a tribune (junior commander).

Next, they might be given the command of a whole legion, and lead men to

war. Successful commanders were made provincial governors,

reporting straight to Rome. The highest honour was to be promoted to command

an entire army, consisting of many legions, and to plan battles and campaigns.

There were three different types of auxiliaries: cavalry, known as 'alae' (wings), because they were fast-moving, and fought on either side of foot-soldiers in battle; infantry (soldiers who fought on foot); and the 'cohors equitata' – mixed regiments of infantry and cavalrymen.

The Navy also played a part in Roman wars. Ships were used to carry men and horses

to fight in distant lands. For example, Julius Caesar had 600 special landing craft and 28 warships built to help in his invasion of Britain in 54 BC. Caesar's new ships were wider and lower than usual. They could be quickly loaded, and could carry troops right up on to the beaches. This meant soldiers could start fighting as soon as they reached the shore.

Warships were armed with a bronze prow to smash enemy boats, and had wooden towers built on their decks to shelter soldiers firing catapults or arrows.

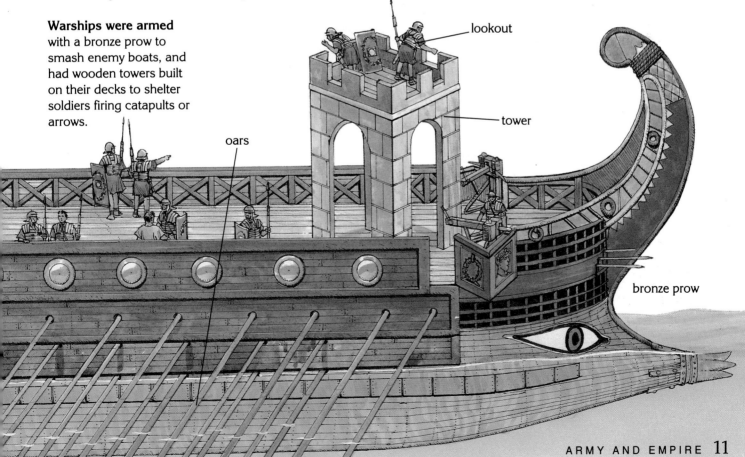

lookout

tower

oars

bronze prow

ROMAN ROADS

a mile post

layer of pebbles
and chippings

stone slabs

stone blocks

raking sand smooth

surveyors

Roman emperors relied on roads to help them
govern their empire. They needed to be able to
send messengers from outlying provinces to
Rome – and back again – quickly and without
accident. They wanted tribute goods and
essential supplies to arrive in Rome safely and in
good condition. They also might have to hurry
large numbers of troops to frontier trouble spots
when rebels threatened.

For all these reasons, the Romans became
expert road-builders and engineers. Roman
roads were built by ordinary soldiers, supervised
by junior officers who were specially trained as
architects, surveyors or procurers of building
supplies. Military architects became famous, and
wrote about building designs and techniques.
Their writings still survive, along with a great
many Roman roads, bridges and other buildings.
Once the army had finished building a new road,
the local community had to maintain it.

Roman roads were planned to suit the army,
not the local people. They were usually made as
straight as possible, and ran between important
towns (where Roman officials were based) and
key military centres, such as forts. Villages and
farms where ordinary men and women lived were
bypassed; they were not important.

Roads were built on
foundations of stone
blocks laid on sand. Layers
of pebbles and stone chips
were added, and covered
with a top surface of stone
slabs or thick gravel.
Drains and kerbs ran along
both sides.

Caspian Sea

Black Sea

Atlantic
Ocean

Mediterranean
Sea

Roman roads (above)
were busy throughout the
empire. So government
and army traffic was given
priority.

Bridges (right) were built
to carry roads and water
supplies. Coffer-dams were
constructed and drained
with Archimedian screws
so that pillars could be
built in rivers and lakes.

Archimedian screw

coffer dam

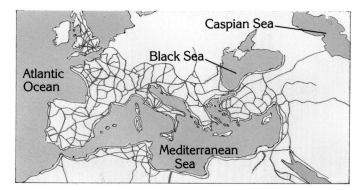

river water

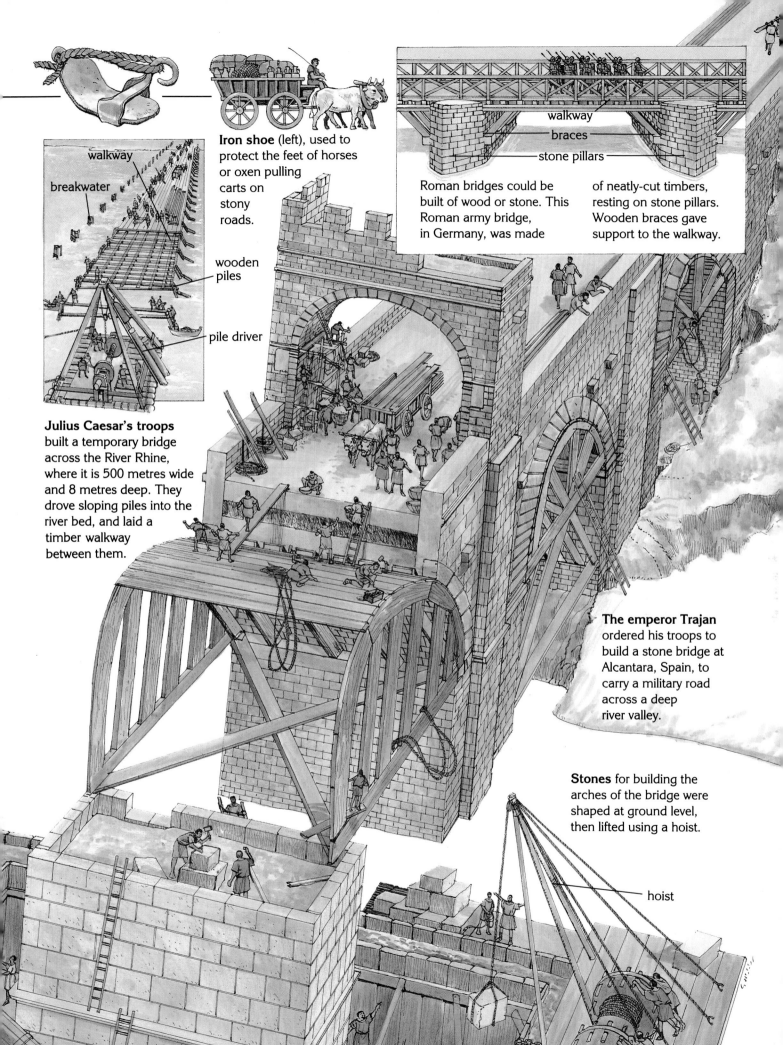

Iron shoe (left), used to protect the feet of horses or oxen pulling carts on stony roads.

walkway

breakwater

walkway
braces
stone pillars

Roman bridges could be built of wood or stone. This Roman army bridge, in Germany, was made of neatly-cut timbers, resting on stone pillars. Wooden braces gave support to the walkway.

wooden piles

pile driver

Julius Caesar's troops built a temporary bridge across the River Rhine, where it is 500 metres wide and 8 metres deep. They drove sloping piles into the river bed, and laid a timber walkway between them.

The emperor Trajan ordered his troops to build a stone bridge at Alcantara, Spain, to carry a military road across a deep river valley.

Stones for building the arches of the bridge were shaped at ground level, then lifted using a hoist.

hoist

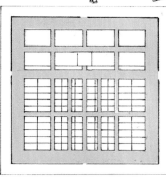

MARCHING CAMPS

The Roman army travelled on foot. Soldiers marched along in strict order – auxiliaries at the front, high-ranking troops safely in the middle, and cavalry at the rear. Each man carried his own armour, weapons and essential kit – a saw, a hook, a rope, a pick-axe, a basket (for shifting earth on building sites), a kettle, a metal food container and toilet articles such as a razor and a comb. Even using well-made Roman roads, heavily-laden soldiers could only travel about 25 kilometres each day. It was therefore necessary to provide somewhere safe and sheltered for the army to rest overnight.

Temporary camps – known as 'marching camps' – were the answer. Here, soldiers slept in

Once a camp site had been found, it had to be defended. If enemies were nearby, half the men stood on guard, while the others dug a ditch (about 3 metres deep and 4 metres wide) to make a square enclosure. Earth was piled up to build a steep rampart.

centurions' tent

Early layout (above) of a marching camp, described by the historian Polybius in the 2nd century BC. The army's leather tents (left) were long-lasting and waterproof. When not in use, they could be rolled up into compact bundles. Tents and tent-poles were carried in ox-carts or on mules.

tent-pegs

commander's tent

legionaries' tent

tents made of leather stretched over wooden poles, with straw covering the floor. Eight men crowded into each tent, which measured about 3 metres square. Officers' tents were bigger.

Around 800 tents were needed to shelter a whole legion. To avoid chaos as night fell and soldiers hurried to unpack, it was important that tents were pitched in neat rows. Camps always had the same layout, wherever the troops were – men boasted they could find their own tent in the dark. The commander's tent was always near the centre of the camp. Legionaries camped behind the commander's tent; tents for auxiliary troops were placed like a 'human shield' between the commander's tent and the enemy.

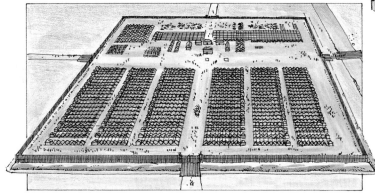

A senior officer, called a tribune, was sent ahead to mark out the site for the camp. He used a white flag to show where the commander's tent should be, and red flags to mark sites for officers and men.

When a century (80 men) was on overnight guard duty, no tents were put up for them. If they fell asleep, they were severely punished, sometimes even executed.

Carving (right) from Trajan's column (see pages 42-43) showing soldiers, wearing cloaks to protect them from the cold, outside a walled camp.

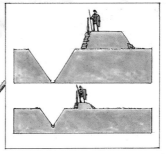

Deep ditch and high rampart (top), used to keep enemies out of the camp. Below: shallow ditch and low rampart, used for a temporary marching camp where there would have been less time to build such a big defence system.

FROM CAMP TO FORT

Marching camps were useful while army units were travelling from one part of the empire to another, or while soldiers were fighting in hostile lands. But once a province had been conquered, or during long drawn-out campaigns, somewhere more permanent was needed for soldiers to live in and use as a base. Forts were built to meet this need.

A typical fort was laid out in a regular grid pattern, like many Roman towns. Buildings were linked by wide roads, leading from the headquarters and the commander's house to the four main gates.

In many ways, a fort was like a larger, stronger marching camp built in wood or stone. (Compare the layout of the fort shown on these pages with the plan of the marching camp on page 14.) Like a camp, a fort provided sleeping accommodation, headquarters offices, and a commander's residence. But a typical fort had many other buildings. No two forts were exactly the same, but most had barracks, baths, lavatories, stables, granaries, kitchens, workshops, a shrine with altars, storerooms, a parade ground, a treasury and a hospital. Some forts had a temple and a sports arena nearby.

Historians have identified two main types of fort: auxiliary garrisons (purpose-built to house fighting troops on active campaigns) and permanent legionary bases (designed to be lived in by regular troops in peace as well as in war). But whichever type they were, all forts were guarded by deep ditches and a strong surrounding wall, with tall watchtowers and well-defended gates.

Via Decumana

Via Praetoria

1
2
3
4
5
8
10
11
12
12
12
13
15

Inside the fort:

1. Porta decumana (back gate).
2. Defensive earthworks (ditch and rampart), topped by a strong stone wall.
3. Watchtower.
4. Workshops.
5. Stores.
6. Bathhouse (with furnace for heating water).
7. Hospital.
8. Additional workshops and/or barns and stables.
9. Praetorium (commander's house).
10. Principia (headquarters building). This housed a shrine, weapons stores, meeting hall, offices for all the officers and clerks running the fort, a treasury, and the room where the standards were kept.
11. Granaries.
12. Barracks where soldiers slept.
13. Side gates.
14. Lavatories.
15. Porta praetoria (main gate).

Outside the fort:

16. Exercise halls where soldiers could do marching drill and practise fighting in bad weather.
17. Civilian settlement or 'vicus', where traders, craft workers, innkeepers and soldiers' families lived.

Forts and walls kept the soldiers safe from enemy attack. They also marked the limits of Roman power, and separated areas of Roman influence from the rest of the non-Roman world. Up until AD 117, Roman armies had been (in the words of one recent historian) 'specialists in expansion'. After that, their task changed: they became defenders. This could be boring, depressing work. Building forts and walls helped keep men busy, and encouraged them to feel proud of what they had achieved. Better living conditions – forts were much more comfortable than camps – also helped to keep up the army's morale while the men were so far from home.

CHOOSING THE SITE

Although they all developed from the basic army camp, not all forts looked alike. Much depended on local conditions – was the ground flat or hilly, rocky or damp? What stone, timber or other building materials were available?

Roman architects, engineers and surveyors took great care to find the best site on which to build. The ideal position for a fort was close to a well-made road, with good supplies of food (for humans and animals), fresh water and timber nearby. It should be easy to defend and have a commanding view of the countryside all around, so that advancing enemies could be seen in time. And, as the Roman author Vegetius pointed out: 'attention must be paid to the healthiness of the place'.

Not surprisingly, this ideal site was rarely found, but Roman builders did their best in many unpromising environments – like the bleak, windswept hills along the Scottish border.

Once the decision to build a fort was taken, all the trees and bushes were cut down. This was an enormous task. The buildings of a large fort covered about 1.5 hectares, but an area of anything up to 6 hectares might need to be cleared, to give the builders room to work. Then the architects and surveyors moved in, to take measurements, work out quantities of materials that would be needed, draw up plans and mark the position of ditches, ramparts, and buildings.

The legion's commander, called a legate, would discuss plans for a fort with government officials and senior army officers. He might also consult written accounts of earlier campaigns, or look at improved designs for forts before building began.

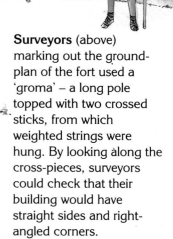

Surveyors (above) marking out the ground-plan of the fort used a 'groma' – a long pole topped with two crossed sticks, from which weighted strings were hung. By looking along the cross-pieces, surveyors could check that their building would have straight sides and right-angled corners.

Legionary and auxiliary soldiers (left) cut down trees and carted timber to build walls around the fort, and some of the inside buildings as well. This was rough, heavy work.

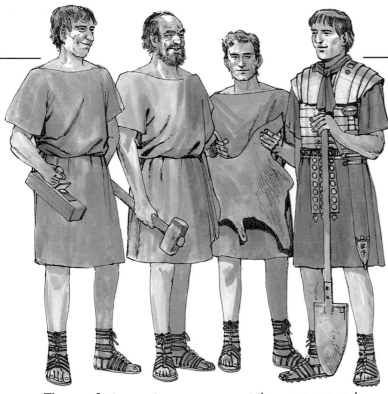

The praefectus castrorum (supervisor) gave orders to all the skilled workmen in the legion. They were classed as 'immunes'. That meant they were excused from routine duties because they had special skills, unlike the ordinary labourers.

Senior officers kept a close watch on building costs. Each legion had a staff of clerks who kept detailed accounts of all the money spent on building a new fort. Once a fort was in use, they also checked the cost of all major building repairs.

It is likely that merchants from conquered peoples sometimes preferred to make money by selling stone and timber to the Romans than to stay loyal to their own leaders who were fighting for freedom from Roman rule.

Friendly local chieftains in parts of Britain and France could be helpful to soldiers building forts, and could give them useful information. They had expert knowledge of local conditions, and also knew the best places to obtain building supplies.

BUILDING THE FORT

Building work was supervised by an official called the 'praefectus castrorum'. He was responsible for carrying out the surveyors' instructions and for making sure that labourers were supplied with all the proper tools. A legion normally included men skilled in many construction tasks, including ditch-diggers, glaziers, tile makers, plumbers, stonemasons, limeburners and woodcutters.

Each legion had its own way of organising building work, and used its own designs for features such as doorways and gates. Some legions fighting in Germany seem to have had a set of ready-made blueprints drawn up, only needing to be adapted to local conditions. At first, auxiliaries were not trusted to work on permanent buildings like forts, although they dug ditches and ramparts around the big camps, and were used by the legions to provide unskilled labour. Later, after about AD 120, auxiliaries began to undertake building projects on their own.

Forts were built from materials available locally. In the north of England, forts were usually made of stone. In the forest lands of Germany, they were made of timber. Sometimes a mixture of materials was preferred; buildings have been found with stone footings or foundations under walls made of wood, and wattle and daub (woven twigs covered with a layer of mud).

Forts were guarded by gateways, with iron-clad doors 10cm thick. Gateways could be built of wood, concrete (stones, earth, lime and water), or massive stone blocks. Big windows helped the guards keep watch.

Strong walls could be made of logs and turf. A carving from Trajan's Column shows a fort being built.

To build stone walls, a core of rammed earth was covered with shaped stone blocks on either side.

Roman tools:
1. pick; 2. hammers; 3. shears; 4. knives;
5. pincers; 6. hatchets; 7. dividers; 8. calipers; 9. borers;
10. plumb-line weights; 11. hoe.

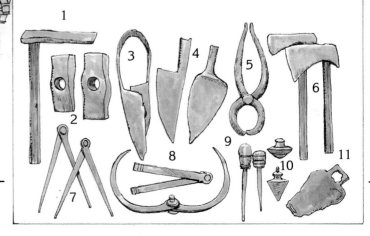

A carved stone records how 'the century of Silvanus built 112 feet (about 34 metres) of rampart'.

Clay antefix (roof ornament) made by men of the XX (20th) Legion, and decorated with a boar.

Lookouts were posted on top of towers. Inside, there were rooms where men could rest between spells on duty.

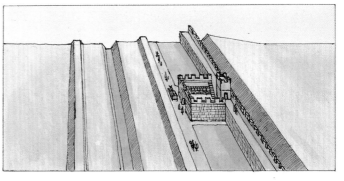

Sometimes the Romans built long, fortified walls, such as Hadrian's Wall in the north of England. It had a ditch, a stone or turf wall with defended gateways (milecastles), and further earthwork barriers.

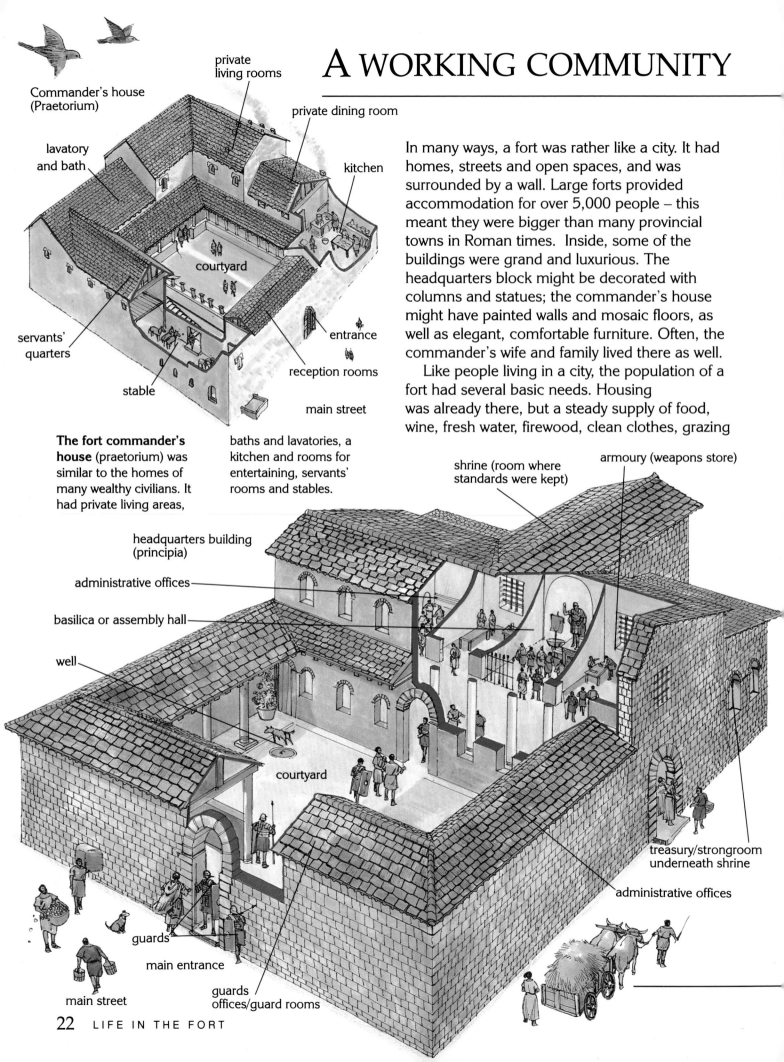

A WORKING COMMUNITY

Commander's house
(Praetorium)

private
living rooms

private dining room

lavatory
and bath

kitchen

courtyard

servants'
quarters

entrance

reception rooms

stable

main street

The fort commander's house (praetorium) was similar to the homes of many wealthy civilians. It had private living areas,

baths and lavatories, a kitchen and rooms for entertaining, servants' rooms and stables.

In many ways, a fort was rather like a city. It had homes, streets and open spaces, and was surrounded by a wall. Large forts provided accommodation for over 5,000 people – this meant they were bigger than many provincial towns in Roman times. Inside, some of the buildings were grand and luxurious. The headquarters block might be decorated with columns and statues; the commander's house might have painted walls and mosaic floors, as well as elegant, comfortable furniture. Often, the commander's wife and family lived there as well.

Like people living in a city, the population of a fort had several basic needs. Housing was already there, but a steady supply of food, wine, fresh water, firewood, clean clothes, grazing

shrine (room where standards were kept)

armoury (weapons store)

headquarters building
(principia)

administrative offices

basilica or assembly hall

well

courtyard

treasury/strongroom
underneath shrine

administrative offices

guards

main entrance

guards
offices/guard rooms

main street

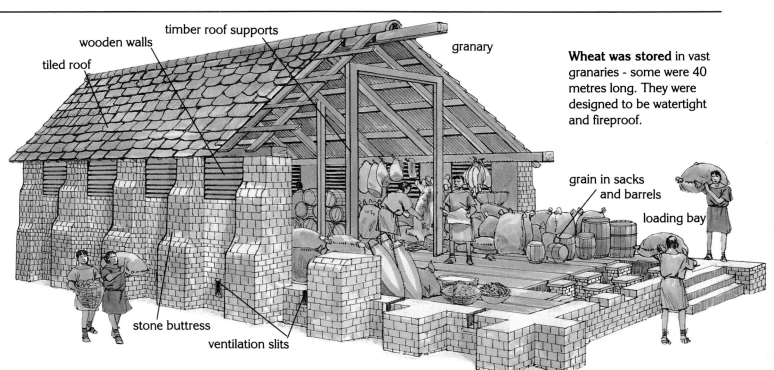

tiled roof
wooden walls
timber roof supports
granary

stone buttress
ventilation slits

Wheat was stored in vast granaries - some were 40 metres long. They were designed to be watertight and fireproof.

grain in sacks and barrels
loading bay

for their horses, and materials to repair their buildings still had to be provided. At different times, they also needed to call on doctors, lawyers, scribes and priests for help and advice.

Towns grew and prospered slowly. But forts were 'instant cities', built in empty countryside, and surrounded by enemy land. Fort-dwellers could not always rely on local merchants, craftsmen or professionals to provide the goods and services they needed straight away. On this page you can see some of the many different people, with many different skills, who worked inside a fort and helped to make it a comfortable place to live.

Granary floors were ventilated to keep grain cool and dry. At one end were bays, where carts could deliver fresh supplies.

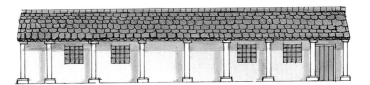

Oats and barley – normally fed to horses – were kept in granaries and store-rooms.

Lazy soldiers were punished by being allowed to eat only barley and water for weeks.

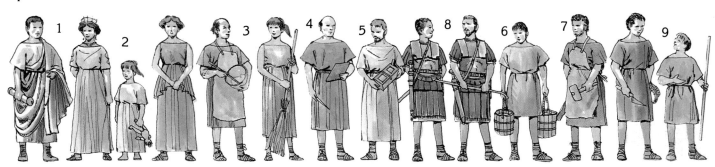

Soldiers were not the only people to live in a Roman fort. A commander (1) brought his wife and family (2) to live with him.

He employed domestic servants (3) to look after the praetoria building and the people who lived there. The army paid clerks (4), doctors (5), grooms (6), blacksmiths (7) and other skilled workers to help army officers (8) run the fort.

Trusted workers from the local community, like this builder and his apprentice (9), also came into the fort each day to work.

WHY BE A SOLDIER?

What made a man become a soldier? The life was tough and the risks were considerable; tombstones from all corners of the empire record the names of soldiers who died in battle, or from diseases caught on campaign. Even when soldiers were not fighting, they spent their time training, or building roads and forts.

Food was simple. A legion on the march ate wheat flour, baked into hard, dry biscuits, and anything else they could find. Discipline was harsh. Soldiers could be flogged for theft – or they might even be crucified. Shared battle experience encouraged trust and comradeship, but men might also feel lonely and isolated. Ordinary soldiers were not allowed to marry, although some had 'unofficial' wives. Sometimes conditions were so bad that troops rebelled.

Why, then, did men enlist? Mainly for the money. Roman soldiers were paid regularly and fairly well and often managed to save part of their earnings. They were also given a share of booty captured in war, and a generous grant when they retired. Before AD 212, some men joined the auxiliaries as a way of improving their position in society; most soldiers were made citizens of Rome when they retired. For a few, there was the chance of promotion, and a responsible career. Perhaps some men joined simply to escape from dull, routine lives. They wanted excitement and a chance to see the world.

Legionary soldiers (above) on campaign in Romania, clearing a path. Carving from Trajan's Column.

Tombstone (right), showing legionary uniform, of a centurion, Marcus Favonius Facilis. He died in about AD 47.

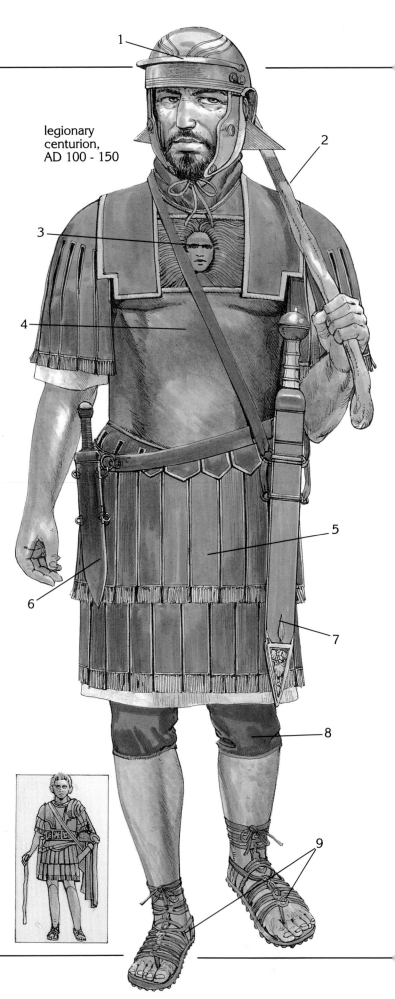

legionary centurion, AD 100 - 150

1
2
3
4
5
6
7
8
9

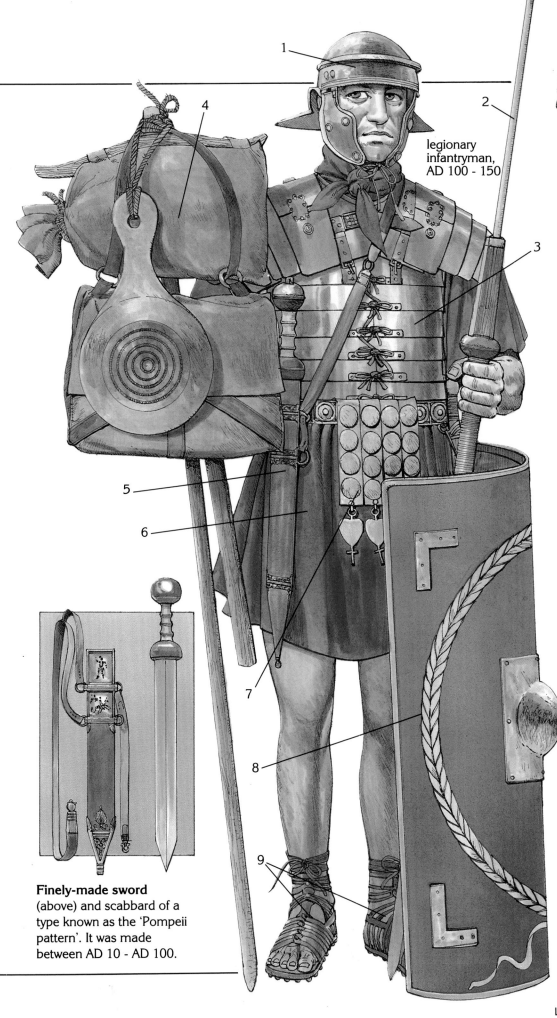

1

4

legionary
infantryman,
AD 100 - 150

2

3

5

6

7

8

9

Putting on underwear
(above) - woollen pants
and a tunic - and fastening
armour. In warm climates,
Roman soldiers did not
normally wear any
underclothes; they thought
they were unmanly. But
soldiers on campaign in
cold northern lands soon
copied local Celtic styles
of clothing to keep warm.

Far left (page 24):
Legionary centurion:
1. Helmet
2. Vine-wood stick
    (sign of rank).
3. Panel with monster's
    head to drive away
    harm.
4. Metal corselet.
5. Leather kilt.
6. Dagger.
7. Sword.
8. Knee breeches.
9. Leather boots.

Left:
Legionary infantryman
1. Helmet.
2. Spear.
3. Corselet of metal
    strips.
4. Essential kit.
5. Sword.
6. Woollen tunic.
7. Leather stomach
    protector.
8. Shield.
9. Leather boots.

Finely-made sword
(above) and scabbard of a
type known as the 'Pompeii
pattern'. It was made
between AD 10 - AD 100.

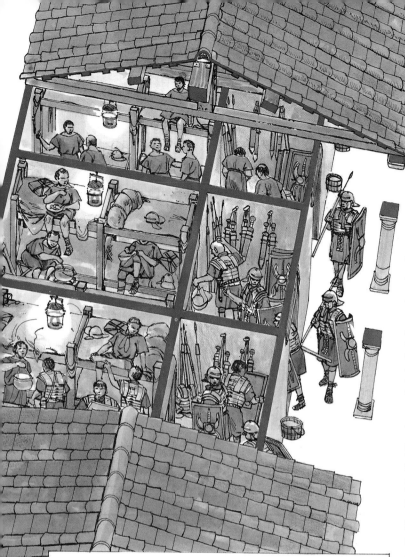

A SOLDIER'S LIFE

Roman soldiers did not spend all their time fighting. But they were still kept busy. There were regular training sessions – including weapons practice every day – to keep troops fit and ready for war. There were reports on the enemy's movements, and briefings from army spies. On festival days, such as the emperor's birthday, there might be a special ceremony, with prayers and sacrifices.

The fort itself had to be guarded. Soldiers patrolled the walls and questioned everyone who entered the gates. They also kept unauthorised people out of the headquarters building and the commander's house.

Reliable men were assigned to special duties, to help local officials keep the peace. A typical provincial governor employed the following extra staff, all 'borrowed' from legions stationed nearby: 3 secretaries, 10 messengers, guards, orderlies, interpreters, torturers, clerks and grooms. Troops were also used as military escorts, customs officers and spies. Lazy soldiers might be given unpleasant duties or 'fatigues': cleaning lavatories and drains.

But for most men in a fort, life was centred on the two rooms in a barrack block which they shared with seven others. They cooked, ate and relaxed together. For soldiers away from home, these close comrades must have been as important as their families.

The layout of legionary barrack blocks developed from the arrangement of soldiers' tents in a marching camp. In a camp, the 10 tents needed to house a complete century (80 men) were pitched together in a row, with the officers' tents at one end. Legionary barrack blocks were similar. They contained 10 pairs of rooms, where the soldiers slept and stored their kit. One pair of rooms was shared between 8 men; one room was used for sleeping, the other for storage and for cleaning and mending equipment. At one end of the block, there were larger rooms, for the centurion.

We can find out about Roman soldiers from their tombstones. For example, this memorial stone gives us a 'mini-biography' of one soldier. His name was Gaius Saufeius, and he served with the IX (9th) Legion, which was active in Britain around AD 65. Gaius died when he was 40 years old, after 22 years of army service, so he must have joined up when he was 18.

Gets up in room shared with 7 other men. Puts on armour. Notices hole in woollen tunic; mends it.

Goes to bakehouse to collect bread for himself and room-mates. Usually they eat together.

Ready for duty. Reports to his centurion, who inspects men for smartness and readiness to work.

On patrol in the country nearby. Has to keep a sharp lookout for anything suspicious.

His 'watch' (period of duty) ends. Goes to see troops at weapons practice on the parade-ground.

Goes to headquarters building to check duty rosters and find out his tasks for next few days.

Goes to one of the fort workshops to collect spare sword that is being mended. Pays for the work.

Meal with room-mates; bread, cold bacon and cheese, lentils and onions, sour wine mixed with water.

Plays quick game of dice with friends. Accuses one of cheating; quarrels. Centurion investigates.

On guard duty again, this time checking everyone who comes and goes by the main gate.

Off duty again. Goes to the fort hospital to visit sick friend, who has broken leg falling off ladder.

Dictates letter to one of the fort clerks to send to injured friend's family, saying friend is ill.

Just time to leave the fort to go to the tavern in the 'vicus' for evening meal and some warm wine.

Looks at nuts and honeycomb offered for sale by local pedlar to soldiers in the tavern.

Returns to fort, wrapped in thick woollen cloak made by local weavers. He will wear it again on night duty.

Back inside barracks room. Centurion checks all men are home. Has short sleep, then on duty again.

FOOD AND WATER

What did Roman soldiers eat? Their basic food was wheat, ground up and mixed with water and cooked to make biscuits, porridge or bread. But wheat by itself was not enough. One Roman author, Vegetius, recognised that it needed sharp flavours to go with it. 'Let them have ... wine, vinegar and salt, in plenty at all times,' he advised. Other Roman experts were concerned about nutrition. They suggested adding lentils, cheese, bacon, lard, vegetables, honey and olive oil to the basic ration of grain. Remains of other tasty foods – rabbits, grouse and deer, fish and fish sauce, oysters, beans, fruits and nuts – have been found at fort sites. These were obtained locally, or imported by merchants.

At camp (above), soldiers cooked food for themselves and for the other 7 members of their contubernium.

Army clerks (below) kept records of foodstuffs purchased and consumed at the fort.

List of army stores (above) written on a wooden tablet. Left: Cooking pot on a stand with an oil-burner to keep food warm.

Wheat (above) and other grains were milled at the fort using millstones turned by mule-power.

Wax tablets (left) and stylus, used for noting rations issued. Steelyard (bottom) used to weigh soldiers' biscuits.

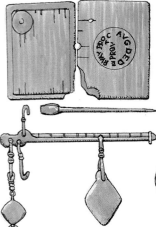

It was important (left) for soldiers at the fort to stay friendly with some local farmers who sold food.

Long-handled metal skillet (above), used by soldiers to cook their food over an open fire.

A good water supply was one of the most important assets a fort could have. Each man needed about 2.5 litres a day. Workshops, baths, and stables used more. Surveyors planning a fort looked for a fast-flowing stream or spring nearby, or, if necessary, dug a well. They channelled the water around the fort, using stone gutters or pipes of lead, wood and clay.

Water went first of all to a fountain, where it was used to fill buckets for drinking and cooking, then to the bath-house, and finally to the lavatories. Where possible, these were built at the lowest point of the fort, so that sewage could flow naturally away. This was a wise precaution, because, as Roman architects warned: 'Dirty water is a kind of poison, and the cause of epidemic disease'.

Roman lavatories (above) could seat several people at once. Seats were placed over a deep channel, flushed with running water. Soldiers used washable sponges on sticks instead of toilet paper.

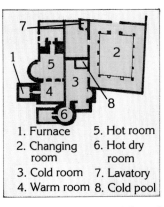

1. Furnace
2. Changing room
3. Cold room
4. Warm room
5. Hot room
6. Hot dry room
7. Lavatory
8. Cold pool

Bath-house (above) found at Red House, near Hadrian's Wall. Built for a fort of the first century AD.

Oil flask (right) and two strigils (scrapers) used at the baths.

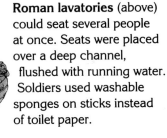

At the baths: Bathers stored their clothes in cupboards built into the changing room wall.

Bathers went first to the cold room, then moved slowly into the warm and hot rooms.

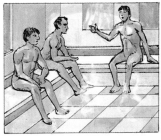

The warm room was heated by steam produced when water was splashed on its hot floor.

Next the hot room made bathers sweat. They had to wear sandals or the floor burnt their feet.

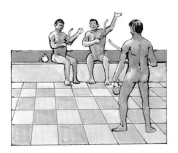

Bathers put oil on their skin and used strigils to scrape it off together with their sweat and dirt.

Then they went back to the cool room, to cool off, and stop sweating. Here they could sit and relax.

Finally they jumped into the cold plunge pool, to rinse their skin. Now they felt clean and fresh.

ILLNESS AND INJURY

Only fit, strongly-built men were accepted as recruits for the Roman army. But even the healthiest of troops could be injured in battle, or develop a serious disease. Each fort had a team of medical staff trained to provide emergency treatment and hospital care. Preventive medicine was important, too. Army officers were responsible for making sure their men kept clean, and, as we have seen, forts were sited and laid out to reduce the risk of disease.

Army doctors were respected, but did not rise to the highest ranks. Doctors were assisted by 'dressers' (given this name because they dressed men's wounds in battle), who also nursed sick soldiers while they recovered. All the medical staff were male. Doctors and dressers worked in large, well-planned hospitals, which were an essential part of every fort.

Roman medical texts describe treatments for a large number of wounds, including jagged cuts from swords, broken bones, dislocated joints, and spear points or arrowheads sunk deep into the flesh. Doctors operated without anaesthetics (except alcohol), but they did know about keeping wounds clean, closing cuts with stitches, amputating mangled limbs and using simple antiseptics such as salt, turpentine, arsenic and oil. Even so, many patients died. Soldiers who recovered, but who were too weak to fight again, were retired with a pension.

Lead stopper from a jar of medicine, containing 'British Root', believed to be a cure for scurvy.

Dresser giving first aid to a wounded soldier on the battlefield. Carving from Trajan's Column.

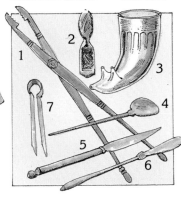

One of the most common and difficult operations was removing weapons from deep wounds (right).

Roman soldiers were trained to face death bravely. They knew that even in hospital, many illnesses could not be cured.

Roman medical instruments:
1. Forceps with toothed grip used for pulling arrows out of wounds.
2. Probe for wide, shallow wounds.
3. Glass dropper for eye treatment or for giving medicine to patients.
4. Bronze spatula (flat knife) for spreading ointment.
5. Knife used in operations.
6. Bronze spatula.
7. Bronze tweezers.

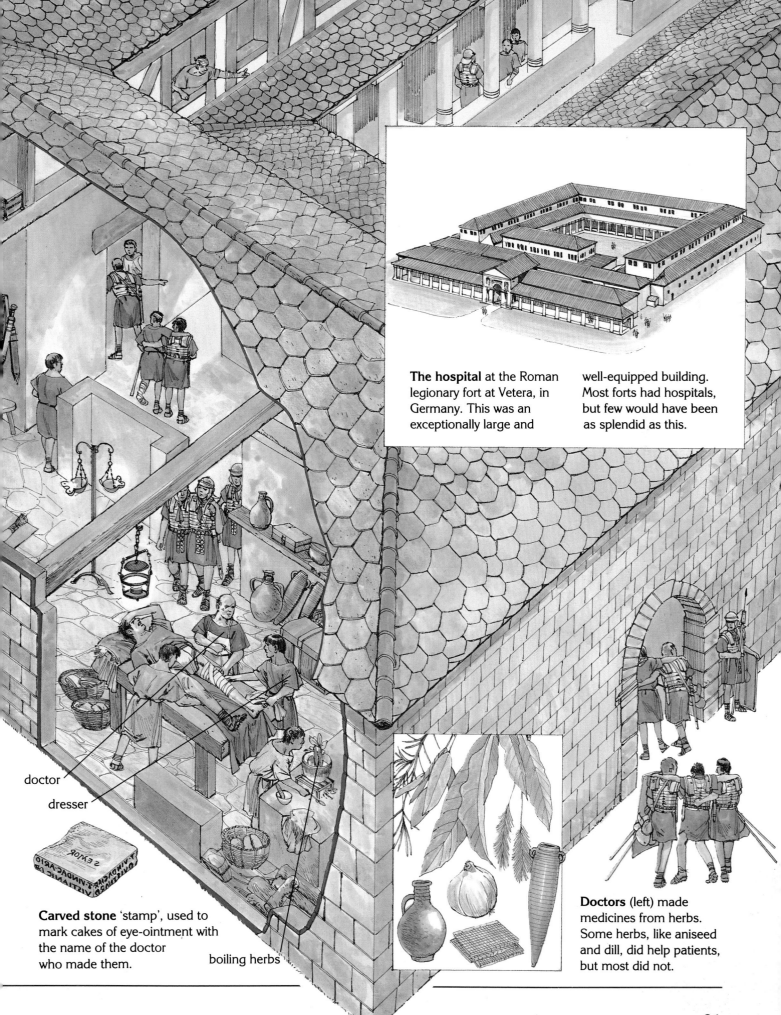

The hospital at the Roman legionary fort at Vetera, in Germany. This was an exceptionally large and well-equipped building. Most forts had hospitals, but few would have been as splendid as this.

doctor

dresser

Carved stone 'stamp', used to mark cakes of eye-ointment with the name of the doctor who made them.

boiling herbs

Doctors (left) made medicines from herbs. Some herbs, like aniseed and dill, did help patients, but most did not.

GODS AND SPIRITS

To Roman soldiers, the world could be a terrifying place. Death could strike at any time, and snatch a soldier's soul. Invisible spirits lurked all around, and ancient gods and goddesses looked down from heaven to judge the actions of mortal men and women.

These mysterious spirits and remote gods played an important part in human affairs. They brought triumph or disaster, so it was important not to offend them. Soldiers made sacrifices of animals or food, hoping to win favour. They also made promises of future offerings if, for example, they survived a battle safely, or had good luck.

The army had its own special gods, which it worshipped at festivals throughout the year. Mars was the god of war, and Jupiter protected governments. Altars dedicated to them, to Hercules, a warlike hero, and to the goddesses Victory and Epona (protector of horses), have been found at many forts.

As well as these long-established religious traditions, there were new, mystery cults which spread throughout the empire from the Middle East. Today, Christianity is the best-known of these, but in Roman times, the worship of Mithras was more popular with soldiers. This was understandable. Mithraism promised comradeship here on earth, and a glorious life after death to men who were killed in war.

Stone carving (above), showing a scene from the life of Mithras. He is shown here sacrificing a bull; its blood was a symbol of everlasting life.

Bronze statue (right) of Mars, the ancient Roman god of battles. It was dedicated 'to Mars and the emperor's divine power'.

This carving (above) of three local gods – the spirits of healing, fertility and life after death – was found near a Roman fort.

Gold ring (above), with a Christian inscription: 'Senecianus, may you live in God'.

The legion's shrine (left) housed statues and altars for the army's 'official' worship of the emperor and the gods of war. It also had a secret strongroom in which valuable objects were hidden.

Statue of Brigantia (above), a north British goddess portrayed in Roman style.

Silver box and wine-strainer (below), perhaps used in religious ceremonies.

Soldiers (right) who had joined the cult of Mithras worshipped in a dark, underground temple, known as a Mithraeum. Senior members of the cult dressed as magical birds and animals, who figured in stories associated with Mithras's achievements.

Scene from Trajan's Column, showing legionary soldiers on campaign taking part in a religious procession. They are leading animals – an ox, a sheep and a boar – which will be sacrificed to the gods in the hope of winning a victory.

OUTSIDE THE WALLS

The army often took over an area of land around a fort where crops could be grown and animals grazed. Sometimes the soldiers farmed this themselves, but, more often, they arranged for local labourers to cultivate it.

One historian has suggested that a Roman fort acted 'like a magnet', attracting merchants from miles around. Excavations have also revealed clusters of new settlements close to Roman forts. In warm countries like Africa and the Middle East, traders lived in tents, spreading their goods on the ground, where soldiers could stroll past and inspect them. In colder lands, new villages grew up, close to the fort's walls.

What happened when a Roman fort was built? What impact did it make on the local community? At first there might have been hostility, but soon local people came to realise that there was money to be made from the newly-arrived soldiers, and began to co-operate. Some local chiefs made alliances with Rome to help them fight against their rivals nearby.

Local sculptors made fine carved tombstones to commemorate soldiers and their families who died while at the fort.

Fragments of several different types of pottery have been found at Roman forts. Simple pots and dishes, for everyday use, were locally made. High-quality, decorated wares were imported from specialist potters in Italy and elsewhere.

Villagers provided all kinds of goods and services, from food, clothes and weapons to taverns and brothels where the soldiers relaxed off duty. Some soldiers also rented houses, where they spent as much time as they could with the local women they had chosen as their wives, and with their children. Officially, the army did not recognise these marriages, but everyone else did.

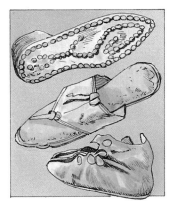

Roman soldiers wore leather boots (like openwork sandals) and shoes. Soles were made from layers of leather, fastened together with iron studs. Boots and shoes needed repairing, so cobblers in the vicus were kept busy.

Cloth for cloaks and tunics was made from wool. Local women spun yarn and wove cloth. Men worked as dyers and tailors.

ON PARADE AND OFF-DUTY

Many forts had a large open space within their walls, close to the headquarters building. This was the parade-ground, used for regular parades and kit-inspections, and also for religious ceremonies on special holy days.

Why did the army hold parades? They were good training, because they helped new recruits learn discipline, and how to recognise urgent battle commands. Parades were also held to teach men to be proud of their legion, and to honour its standard. Commanders, officers, men and even horses wore their best uniforms, and looked on respectfully as the standards were carried by.

A standard was a legion's symbol. It was made from a long metal pole decorated with emblems, often covered in gold. Some legions had a totem animal, like a boar or a wolf. Little statues of these were fixed to the standards.

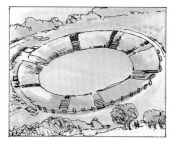

The amphitheatre (above) close to the Roman fortress at Caerleon, Wales. It was built around AD 80.

The top of a standard, carried on parade. The hand shows it belonged to a maniple (160 men).

Officers on parade (below) – and their horses – wore special ceremonial armour, made of gold or silver. It was too valuable and delicate to wear in war.

Beautifully-decorated metal chamfrons or face-masks, (below and left), made for auxiliaries' horses to wear at special parades. Both these examples were found in southern Germany.

These polished metal face masks (far left) were worn by auxiliary soldiers giving marching and riding displays.

Ceremonial parades might also be held in sports arenas (called amphitheatres) outside the fort. Then, when most of the soldiers were off-duty, they would often be followed by some kind of entertainment. Gladiators were popular with Roman audiences, but too expensive for most garrisons to hire. Local wild animals might be chased and killed, or enemy prisoners, too weak to be sold as slaves, might be made to fight until they died. Other popular sports included chariot-racing and wrestling.

Roman soldiers (below) marched long distances carrying heavy loads, and laboured to build camps and forts. This helped keep them fit for battle. But daily weapons practice was even more important. Soldiers fought with padded armour and blunted swords. But if they fought carelessly, they could still get hurt.

Gaming board (above left) made of stone, with glass counters.

Board (above right) for ludus latrunculorum.

Mosaic showing chariot racing (above), found in Lincolnshire. Racing was risky, for men and horses, but it attracted huge crowds of spectators. They liked to bet on who would win.

Soldiers (below) played 'ludus latrunculorum', a game like modern draughts.

IN BATTLE

Roman soldiers were good at fighting; that was what they were paid for. They were brave, fit, loyal and well-armed. But this could also be said of many of the troops they fought and conquered. Why was the Roman army so successful against so many strong and courageous foes?

The Roman army won battles partly because Rome was rich. The government of the empire could afford to keep a large army permanently ready to fight. It could also afford to build good roads and special ships to rush troops quickly to wherever they were needed.

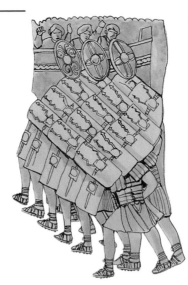

Soldiers overlap their shields to make a testudo (tortoise) – a strong, defensive 'shell'.

An auxiliary archer. Arrows could travel further than javelins, allowing the army to attack at long range.

Legionary soldiers in the front line hurl spears at the enemy. A strong soldier could throw a javelin to wound an enemy over 25 metres away. Their comrades stand behind them, ready to follow up with a second wave attack.

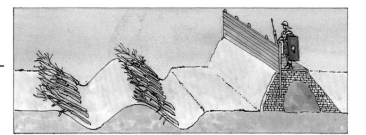

Forts (above) were given extra defences by filling the surrounding ditches with spiky thorn branches.

Seventeen forts (below) were built along the Roman frontier at Hadrian's Wall in northern England.

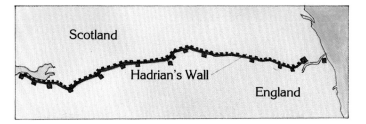

Scotland

Hadrian's Wall

England

The Romans also won battles because commanders planned campaigns with intelligence and skill. Roman strategists and tacticians had an almost 'scientific' attitude to war. They believed it was no use simply to let soldiers charge headlong against an enemy; instead, commanders should consider the layout of a battlefield, the direction of the wind and even the time of day. Caesar, one of Rome's best generals, advised his soldiers to attack when the sun was behind them, so that its bright rays would dazzle and confuse the enemy.

The Roman army also used manpower cleverly. Armies were made up of men trained to fight in many different ways. Together, they worked more effectively than an army of non-specialists, however brave they might be.

This thorough training meant that in an emergency, Roman commanders could rely on their soldiers to act quickly and sensibly.

Portable artillery (above), like this ballista, is used to shoot metal bolts at enemy targets.

Ballista bolt (above) in the spine of a British warrior, who died defending a Celtic stronghold.

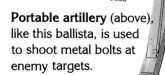

Now they have thrown their spears, soldiers move closer to the enemy and fight 'hand-to-hand' using swords. Usually, only the sharp tip of the sword is used, to cut and wound.

Roman soldiers fought many battles against the Celtic peoples who lived in Britain, France and Germany. The Celts were brave fighters, but were used to attacking in chariots or on horseback. They were not as skilled as Roman soldiers when fighting on foot.

SIEGE WARFARE

wooden arm

onager

Roman forts were built to 'hold' a frontier – which might be marked by no more than a road – against hostile people. Enemies could usually be driven off, thanks to a fort's strong walls. But sometimes a frontier had to be abandoned if it was in very open surroundings and proved too difficult to defend.

twisted rope

An onager (above). Rocks are loaded into a sling fixed to a wooden arm. This will be winched backwards by twisting a rope. When the rope is loosed, the wooden arm shoots forwards, hurling out the rocks.

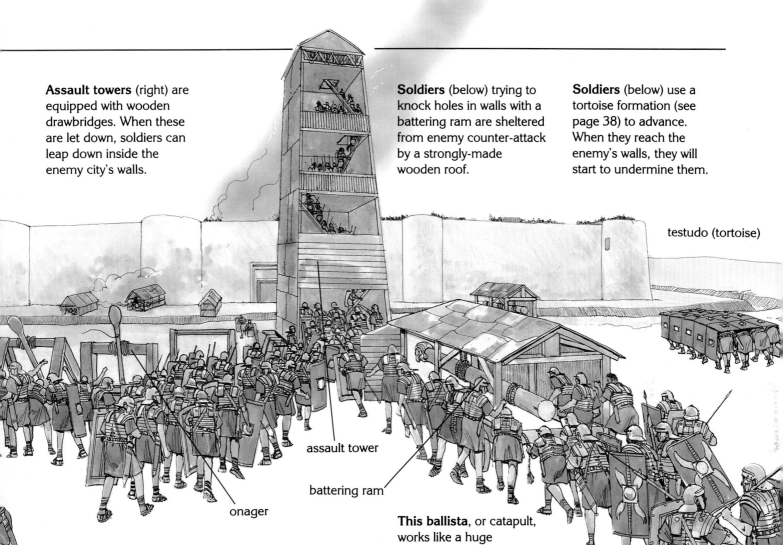

Assault towers (right) are equipped with wooden drawbridges. When these are let down, soldiers can leap down inside the enemy city's walls.

Soldiers (below) trying to knock holes in walls with a battering ram are sheltered from enemy counter-attack by a strongly-made wooden roof.

Soldiers (below) use a tortoise formation (see page 38) to advance. When they reach the enemy's walls, they will start to undermine them.

testudo (tortoise)

onager

assault tower

battering ram

This ballista, or catapult, works like a huge crossbow. Unlike an onager, which takes four men to operate, a ballista only needs two; one loads the flat-tipped metal bolts, the other pulls the lever to release the bow string.

ballista

For example, around AD 158, the Romans demolished a line of forts along the Antonine Wall in Scotland, and retreated southwards to safety. That failure was unusual. More often, forts were successfully used as bases for Romans to launch their own attack. Troops stationed in forts rode out on raiding parties, or staged a carefully-planned ambush. Sometimes sieges were used to conquer hostile towns. In the fort workshops, carpenters and blacksmiths made ingenious war-machines which could be used by Roman troops to smash their enemies.

Few walls were strong enough to stand up to a pounding from a Roman battering ram. Roman military technicians also designed enormous catapults to hurl rocks long distances over enemy walls. They built tall towers, covered with strong wooden cladding, so that soldiers could shoot arrows down into the enemy city, while remaining (fairly) safe themselves.

A LASTING RECORD

An ancient myth told how triumphs originated: after killing a local leader in battle, the Roman king,

Romulus, seized his rich armour, and led the Roman soldiers homeward, singing and dancing. By Trajan's

times, many more people took part in a triumphal procession. It had become a religious, as well as a

military occasion. Only emperors were given triumphs; lesser men had 'ovations'.

The emperor Trajan reigned from AD 98-117. He won important victories in Dacia (present-day Romania), Armenia, Turkey and Iraq. He also started a building programme along the empire's northern frontiers. One of the best-known Roman defences, Hadrian's Wall in the north of England, was not built until after Trajan's death, but he had already started to build forts and roads in that 'danger zone'.

When Trajan returned to Rome in AD 106, he was awarded a 'triumph'. This was an honour given to victorious emperors and their troops. They paraded through the streets of Rome to receive praise and thanks from the citizens.

Heads of Dacian warriors (above) are offered to the emperor Trajan by his victorious troops after a hard-fought battle. Roman troops did not respect the bodies of their enemies, although they held solemn funeral services for their own dead comrades.

The triumphal arch (below) built in Rome to honour the emperor Titus, who ruled from AD 79 - 81.

Triumphal arches (above) were decorated with carving, and with inscriptions praising the general's achievements.

Prisoners were sometimes carried on litters (6), shoulder-high. They were later sold as slaves. In memory of the ceremony's ancient origins, trophies of captured armour (7) were paraded beside them.

Then came the 'triumphator', the man being honoured (8). He rode in a gold-coloured chariot. His face was painted red, he wore kingly robes, and he carried a sceptre and olive branch.

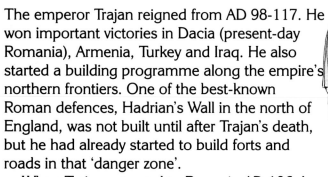

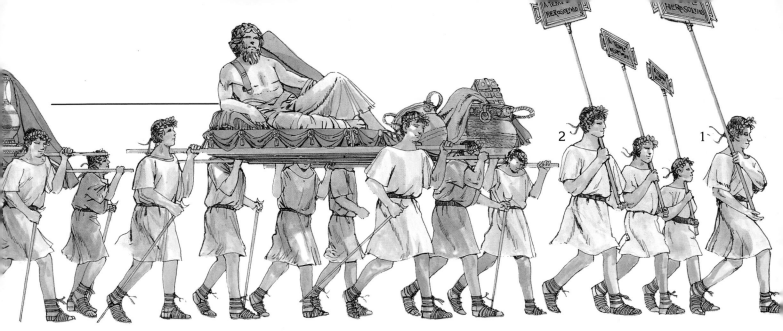

The procession was led by the magistrates and senators – the ruling class of Rome (1) and (2).

They were followed by treasure captured from the enemy (3), or, sometimes, models of conquered cities.

White oxen, chosen for sacrifice, came next (4), along with enemy prisoners in chains (5).

The most important enemy captive was later taken away to be executed, as a sacrifice to the Roman gods.

Often, a beautiful stone arch was built to commemorate their victories, but, to record Trajan's great campaigns, a different monument was chosen.

'Trajan's Column' is a stone pillar, about 30 metres high. It is decorated with a spiral band of carvings, more than 80 metres long. It shows over 2,500 Roman soldiers on campaign marching, fighting and building forts.

For historians today, Trajan's Column provides a very helpful record of Roman army life. But what did it mean to people living at the time? For many Roman soldiers, it must have summed up their aim in life: to work hard, fight bravely and win praise and rewards before they died.

When the triumphal procession (above) reached the Capitol - the sacred centre of Rome - and the chief prisoner had been executed, the general being honoured sacrificed an ox to Jupiter, the greatest Roman god. This scene comes from a silver cup.

Behind the triumphator, in his chariot, stood a slave (9) who whispered to him: 'Remember, in the hour of your triumph, that you are only a man.' The emperor's chariot was followed by his victorious troops (10).

They wore their best uniforms and had laurel wreaths on their heads as they marched.

The soldiers shouted 'Io Triumphe' (Look at the Triumph). They also sang bawdy songs.

ROMAN FACTS

Language and letters

In the glossary on pages 45 - 47, you will see some words in *italics*. These are words in Latin, the language the Romans used. Today, almost 2000 years after most Roman forts were built, many of these words, for example, *'contubernium'*, have almost completely disappeared. This is because the thing they describe (Roman soldiers in a tent) no longer exists. Words like this are now used only by historians and archaeologists studying the Roman past.

But, as you can see, many other Roman words have survived, hardly changed, in the languages we speak today.

Inscriptions and tombstones

Grand inscriptions, like the proud words carved on Trajan's Column (page 42), were written in precise, elegant Latin, which educated Roman people spoke and were able to read. Ordinary Roman soldiers spoke in a simpler style, and some could not read at all. Many auxiliary soldiers, recruited from non-Roman nations, preferred to speak the language of their homeland even while they were serving with the Roman army. Sometimes their tombstones, or those of their families, record soldiers' two languages. For example, Barates, an auxiliary from Syria serving at a fort near Hadrian's Wall, arranged a memorial to his wife. The Latin carving reads: 'To the spirits of the departed and to Regina, his freedwoman and wife, from the Catuvellanian tribe, aged thirty, Barates of Palmyra set this up'. These words are followed by a more personal message, in Barates' own, Syrian, language: 'Regina, the freedwoman of Barates, alas'.

Messages from home

Legionary and auxiliary soldiers used scribes to help them write letters home and, perhaps, to help them read the answers they received. Some of these letters, written on thin strips of wood, have survived. They reveal that soldiers born in warm Mediterranean lands asked for extra warm clothing while serving at northern frontier forts. One letter, sent to a Roman soldier stationed in northern Britain, reads, 'I have sent you two pairs of socks... and two pairs of underpants... greet my friends... and all your mess (room)-mates'. Letters from one fort commander's wife to another have also survived; they show how women tried to maintain contact while living in wild, lonely lands.

GLOSSARY

Altar, a stone 'table' where sacrifices were made.

Amphitheatre, (*Amphitheatrum*) a large building containing many rows of seats where games and other public performances took place.

Antefix, (*Antefixus*) a decorated tile, often placed at the edge of a roof.

Archimedian screw, an ancient Greek invention, used to lift water by forcing it to flow along a spiral-shaped channel cut into the surface of a heavy log, which is kept turning round by a wheel attached to its upper end. Each time the log turns, the water in the channel is moved further along, towards the upper level.

Artillery, weapons that shoot bullets or (in Roman times) arrows and metal bolts.

Asset, something valuable.

Assigned, given to.

Auxiliaries, (*Auxilia*) troops in the Roman army, recruited from non-Roman peoples.

Ballista, a Roman weapon, like a huge crossbow.

Barracks, buildings where soldiers live.

Basilica, a large assembly hall.

Bawdy, rude.

Blueprints, designs for buildings.

Bolt, a metal rod or dart, fired like an arrow.

Booty, treasure captured in war.

Briefing, information and orders given to troops.

Brothels, houses where prostitutes live.

Calipers, tool used to make measurements.

Cavalry, soldiers who fight on horseback.

Celtic, belonging to the native peoples – called Celts – who lived in Britain, northern France and Germany.

Century, a unit in the Roman army: 80 men.

Chamfron, face-armour worn by a horse.

Coffer dam, a strong, heavy, box-shaped structure, built on land and lowered into the water so that it stands on the sea bed or on the bottom of a river or lake. Once the dam is in position, the water inside the 'box' can be pumped out, leaving a dry space for builders.

Cohort, (*Cohors*) six centuries – 480 soldiers.

Commemorate, provide a memorial for.

Contubernium, a group of 8 soldiers who shared a tent or a pair of barrack rooms.

Corselet, armour covering the back, chest and stomach.

Crucified, (*Crucifictus*) put to death by being fixed to a cross.

Cult, (*Cultus*) a way of worshipping gods.

Dislocated, forced out of correct position.

Drawbridge, a wooden bridge that can be raised or lowered by using ropes or chains.

Dressers, people who give 'first aid' in battle.

Emblem, sign or badge.

Enlist, join the army.

Epidemic, disease that is widespread throughout a population.

Fatigues, (*Fatigatio=tiredness*) unpleasant army duties.

Flogged, punished by being whipped.

Footings, stones or strong timbers at the base ('foot') of a wall.

Forceps, medical instruments like pincers, used to grip and remove weapons from wounds.

Garrison, building where an army is based.

Glazier, craft worker skilled at handling glass.

Granaries, buildings where grain is stored.

Gradients, sloping land.

Groma, an instrument (two cross-pieces mounted on top of a pole) used by Roman surveyors to measure straight lines and corners.

Grooms, people who look after horses.

Immunes, soldiers with special skills who were excused from normal army duties.

Imperial, (*Imperatoris*) belonging to an empire.

Infantry, soldiers who fought on foot.

Ingenious, (*Ingeniosus=naturally clever*) cleverly designed and made.

Inscription, (*Inscriptio*) words carved on stone, wood or metal.

Iron-clad, covered with iron.

Javelin, a weapon; a kind of spear.

Landing-craft, boats used to carry an army to the shore.

Laurel, (*Laurus*) an evergreen bush, with shiny leaves. For the Romans a laurel-wreath was a sign of honour.

Legate, (*Legatus*) a man of high rank, who commanded a legion.

Legion, (*Legio*) the most important unit in the Roman army. It contained 10 cohorts - 4,800 soldiers.

Legionary, (*Legionarius*) belonging to, or connected with, a legion.

Limeburner, building worker who made cement.

Litter, (*Lectica*) a portable bed.

Magistrate, (*Magistratus*) government official responsible for administering the law.

Mangled, crushed and broken.

Maniple, (*Manipulus*) two centuries – 160 men.

Milecastle, gateway through Hadrian's Wall.

Mortal, (*Mortalis*) human; bound to die.

Mosaic, picture made from thousands of tiny coloured tiles or fragments of stone. Wealthy Romans liked mosaic floors in their homes.

Onager, a Roman war-machine, which hurled rocks at the enemy. It was named after an onager (a wild donkey), because it 'kicked'.

Orations, (*Oratio*) speeches.

Piles, strong wooden posts used to support buildings, bridges and roads.

Plumber, (*Plumbum=lead*) someone skilled in working with lead.

Plumb-line, a tool used to measure straight lines, made of a string with a heavy weight attached.

Plundering, taking away goods from enemies.

Porta, the Latin word for gate.

Praetorium, the commander's house in a fort.

Praefectus castrorum, the officer responsible for organising the building of a fort or camp.

Principia, the headquarters building in a fort.

Probe, a medical instrument used to feel deep inside wounds.

Procurers, those who buy something on behalf of the organisation they work for.

Province, (*Provincia*) a part of the Roman empire.

Provincial, (*Provincialis*) belonging to a province.

Rammed, hammered down hard.

Rampart, a bank of earth, used as a defence.

Rations, basic food supply.

Recruits, men who have just joined the army.

Sacrifice, (*Sacrificium*) an offering to the gods.

Sarcophagus, a coffin.

Sceptre, (*Sceptrum*) decorated stick, carried as a sign of power.

Scouts, lookouts who go ahead to check that all is clear.

Scribe, (*Scriba*) someone trained to read and write, who uses these skills to make a living.

Senator, a member of the Roman government.

Shrine, a holy place.

Sling, a strip of cloth, used to hurl stones or bolts with great force at the enemy.

Strategists, people who plan army campaigns.

Surveyors, people who make accurate measurements of sites where roads and buildings are to be built.

Tacticians, people who plan how to fight battles.

Testudo, a 'tortoise' battle formation of soldiers with shields (page 41).

Totem, a mascot or guardian animal.

Transylvania, part of present-day Romania and Hungary.

Treasury, a place where valuables are stored.

Tribune, a junior army officer.

Tribunal, (*Tribunus Militaris*) a platform where judges sat.

Tribute, (*Tributum*) goods sent by conquered peoples to their rulers.

Trophies, (*Trophaeum*) precious goods captured in war.

Vallum, a deep defensive ditch.

Ventilated, allowing air to circulate.

Vicus, a civilian settlement by a fort.

INDEX